I AM A SEXUAL BEING

AN ADULT JOURNAL FOR SELF-EXPLORATION

BY
SCOTT SHANNON

Copyright 2016
S.A.S. Publishing
All Rights Reserved

S.A.S. Publishing
99 Second St.
Franklin, NC 28734
(828) 524-0175

If you have purchased a Kindle version of this book please forward a copy of your receipt to scott.shannon62@gmail.com. I will then send you a link for a printable version.

Introduction

This book is full of writing and thinking ideas to help you recognize and celebrate that you are a sexual being who deserves to have a fun and fulfilling sex life.

In working with this journal you may be asked questions or simply see a statement. In either case your response should be to write something (short or long) that these statements or questions inspire or provoke in you. If you need to write more than what you can fit on the page, simply continue your writing on the back of the page. They're all blank.

Sometimes you may react with a painful emotion. But remember, it's OK to feel and express your feelings through laughter or tears, and everything in between. Sex and sexuality can be a controversial topic. This is adult material. It is recommended that you keep this journal private. This will allow you to be completely honest in your responses.

You may go through this journal in the order it is presented or you may skip around as you choose. You're an adult, so, of course, it's up to you. However you use the book it is my sincere hope that you, too, will be a happy sexual being.

You may find it relaxing to color some of the pages using pens or markers. I have intentionally left a blank page behind each journal page. But be sure to put a blank sheet of paper behind the page you are coloring to prevent bleeding onto the next page.

Scott Shannon

Scott Shannon has a Master's degree in Counseling Psychology and fifteen years of experience serving as a sex and relationship therapist to couples, and individuals.

What was your first sexual experience? This could be exploring your body or genitals, masturbating, "heavy petting", or intercourse.

Sex must never be talked about.

Being sexual is dirty.

What is your first memory of yourself as a sexual being?

What was your first sexual experience? This could be exploring your body or genitals, masturbation, "heavy petting", or intercourse.

When did you first know that girls and boys are different?

Being sexual before marriage is a sin.

The "Missionary Position" is the only proper way to have intercourse.

The man in a relationship should always be the one to initiate sexual activity.

Sex must never be talked about.

I still believe everything I was taught about sex.

MY SEXUAL EXPERIENCE

I have engaged in sexual activity in the same room where people are sleeping.

I have engaged in sexual activity in a guest room while visiting friends or family.

I have engaged in sexual activity in the bathroom of a public place.

I have engaged in sexual activity at a club, a bar, or a movie theater.

I have engaged in sexual activity at a party.

I have engaged in sexual activity at a strip club/peep show/X-rated movie theater.

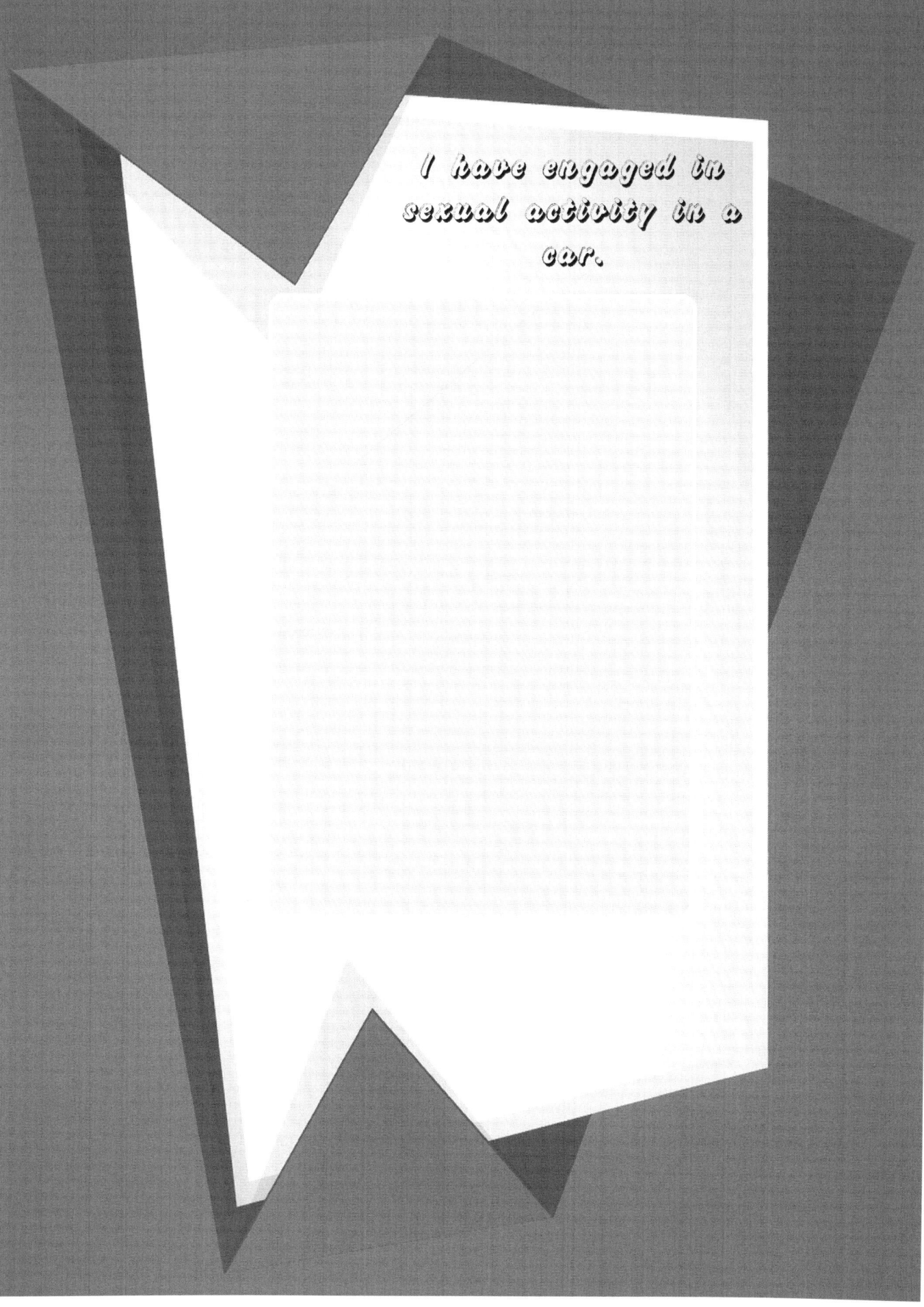

I have engaged in sexual activity in a car.

I have engaged in sexual activity outdoors in a seculded area.

I have many vivid, elaborate, and ever-changing sexual fantasies.

I act out my sexual fantasies.

I act out my sexual fantasies.

My favorite sexual fantasy is . . . ?

I talk about my sexual fantasies with my partner.

I talk about my sexual fantasies with my partner.

I enjoy receiving oral sex.

I enjoy watching pornographic movies with my partner.

I own and wear sexy lingerie or attire.

I use sex toys when I am by myself.

I use sex toys when I am with my partner.

I enjoy giving anal sex (penetration with a penis, finger, or sex toys).

I enjoy receiving anal sex (penetration with a penis, finger, or sex toys).

I enjoy getting undressed while my partner watches.

I am comfortable engaging in sexual activity in bright light or daylight.

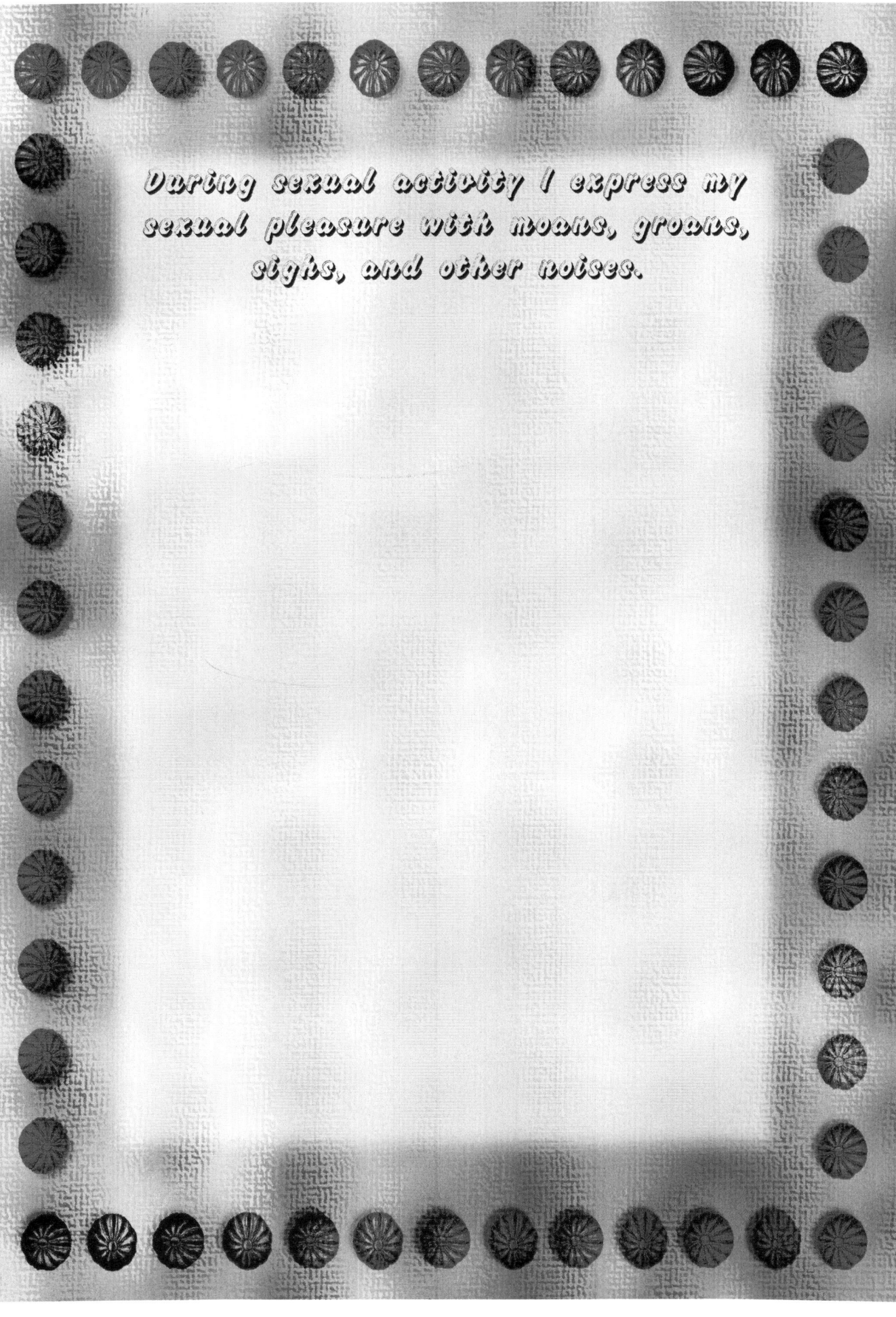

I talk to my partner in a sexually-explicit way.

When do you think that masturbation is OK?

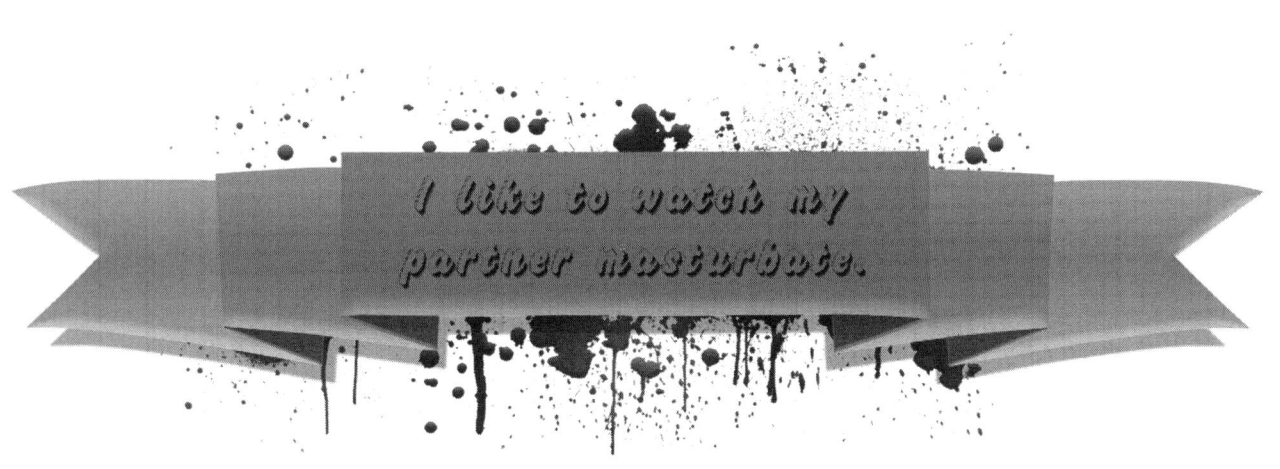

I let my partner watch me masturbate.

I let my partner watch me masturbate.

I tell my partner about my "hot spots".

I like to use many different positions during sexual activity.

I like to engage in role playing games.

I like the idea of spanking during sexual activity.

I like the idea of spanking during sexual activity.

I have engaged in spanking during sexual activity.

I like to watch my partner and me in a mirror during sexual activity.

I enjoy engaging in bondage during sexual activity.

I enjoy having phone sex, or "sexting" with my partner.

How do you feel about "swinging" (having sex with other couples)?

I enjoy having a threesome during sexual activity.

I enjoy having a threesome during sexual activity.

The idea of engaging in sadomasochism turns me on.

My experience with sadomasochism is . . . ?

The idea of sharing the writings in this book with another person is . . . ?

Since I'm a man I can't be cuddly and affectionate.

What happened to the foreplay?

What happened to the foreplay?

My partner won't perform oral sex.

I feel as if my partner takes me for granted.

We just don't have enough sex!

We just don't have enough sex!

SPICE IT UP!

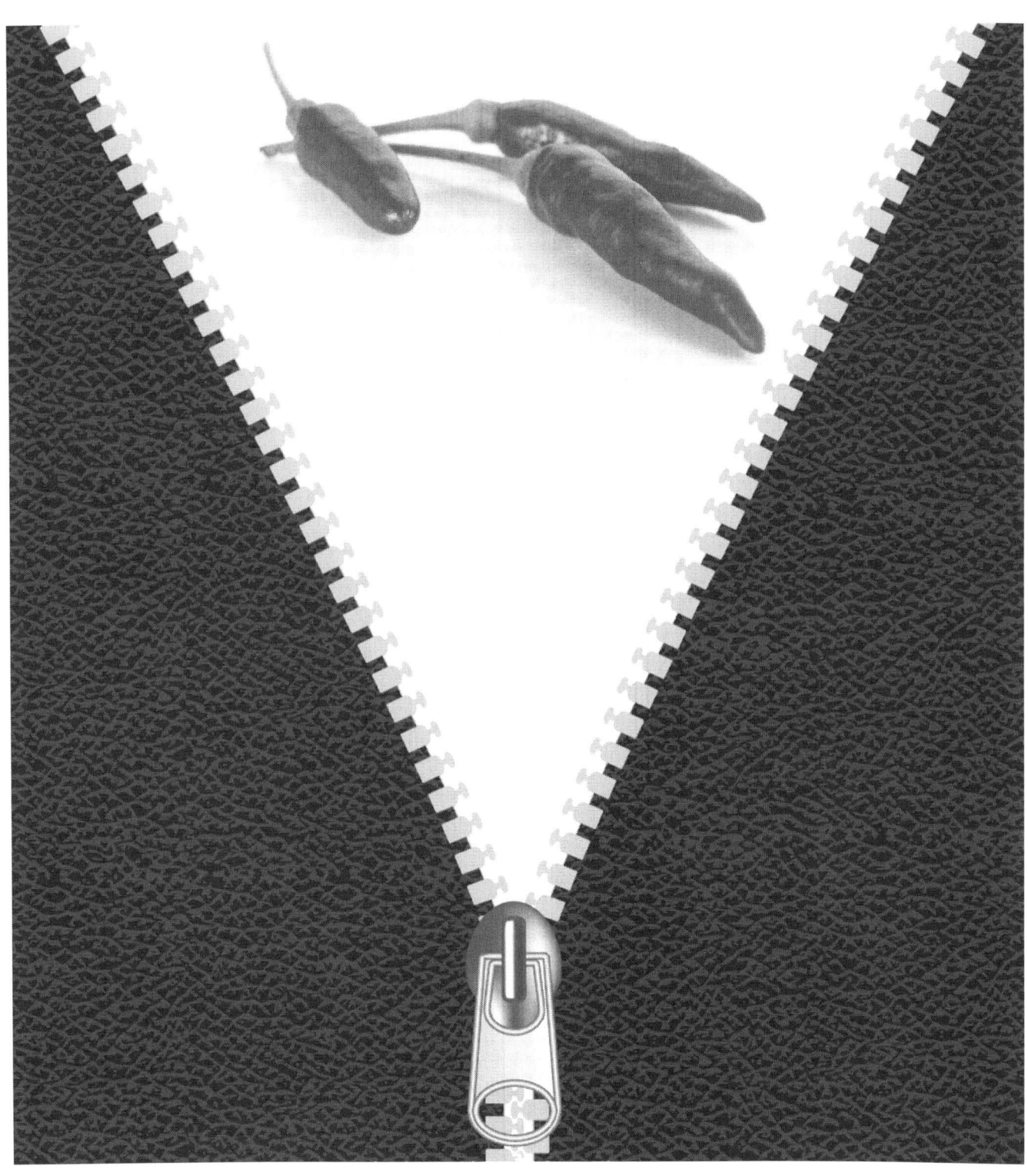

I will view my sexual activity as a time to play, rather than see it as a duty or only a physical release.

I will engage in sexual activity more often.

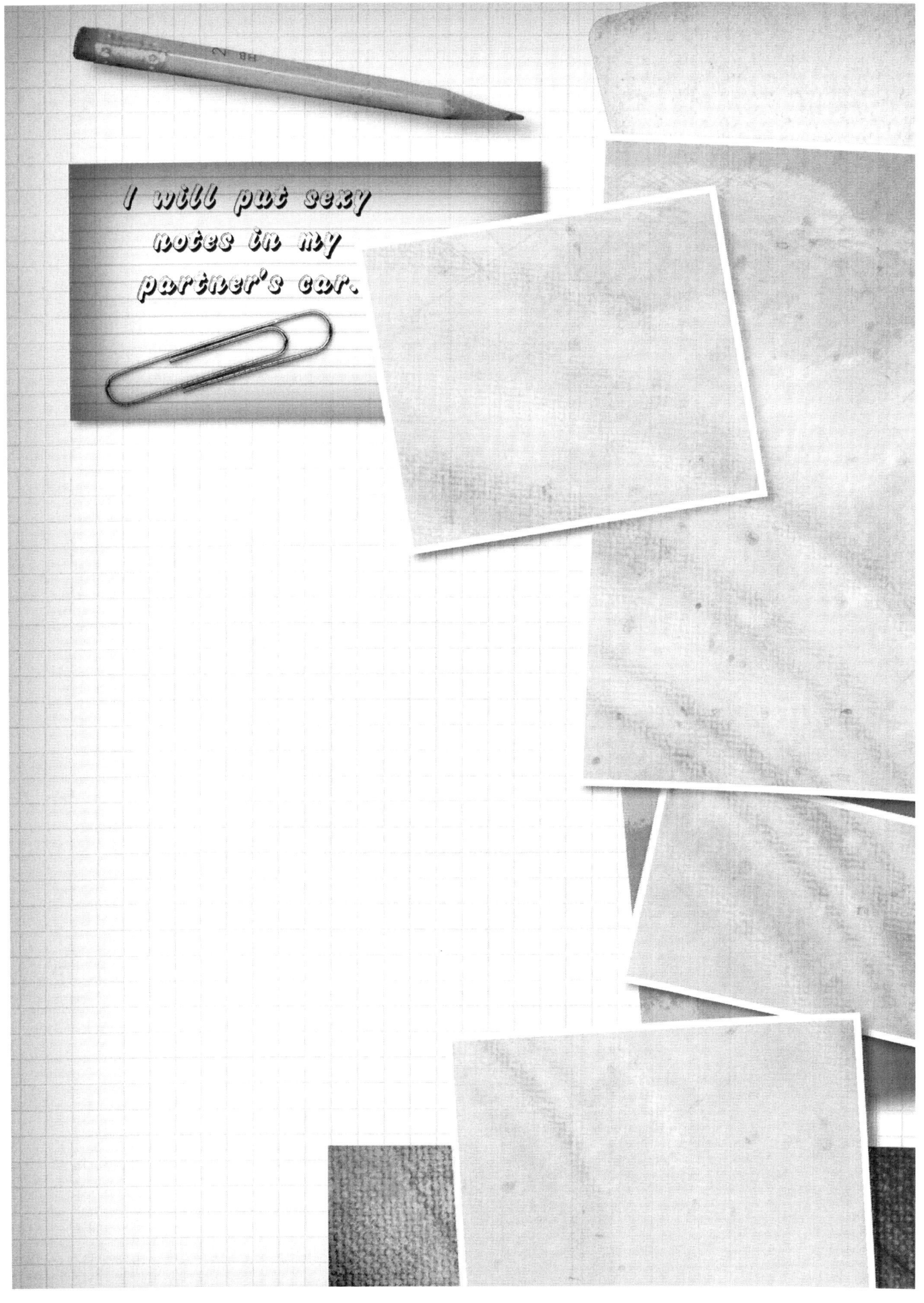

I will flirt with my partner in public.

In public, I will whisper in my partner's ear how much I want sex.

I will do a strip tease for my partner.

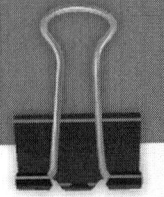 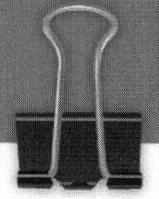

I will engage in sexual activity in a place (hotel, living room, outdoors) other than my bedroom.

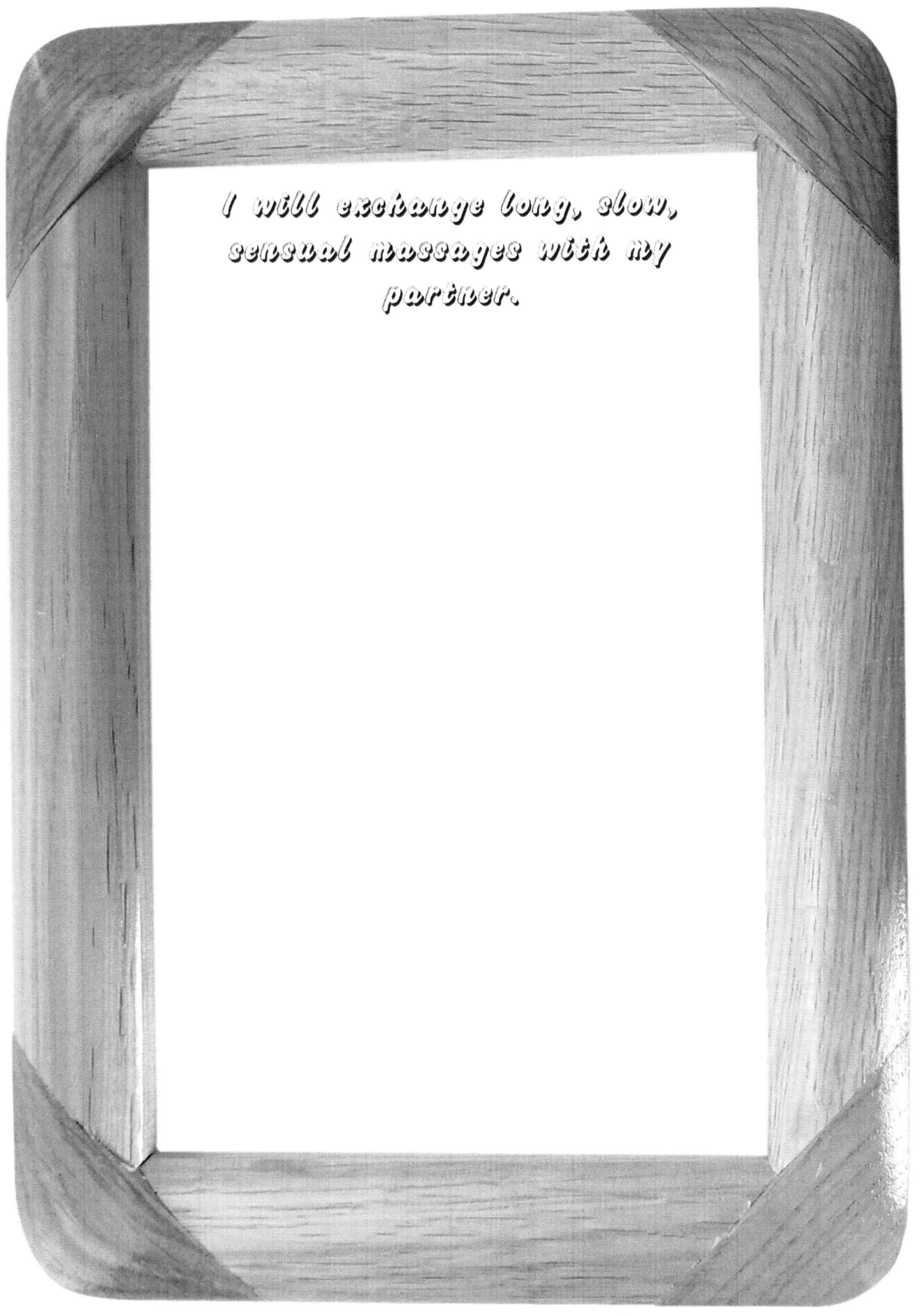

I will exchange long, slow, sensual massages with my partner.

I will masturbate in front of my partner without letting him/her touch me.

MY SEXUAL FUTURE

 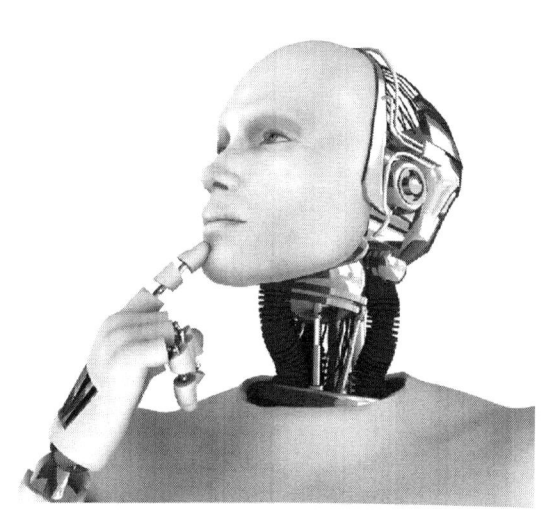

I will talk to my partner about the good/great sexual activity we have had in the past.

I will talk to my partner about the not so good sexual activity we have had in the past and how we may improve it.

During sexual activity I will tell my partner what feels good and how I feel emotionally.

During sexual activity I will ask my partner what feels good and how he/she feels emotionally.

I will be open to trying new things during sexual activity.

I will be open to trying new things during sexual activity.

I will go on a romantic getaway with my partner.

Conclusion

Wow! What a journey. No matter whether you took a short time or a long time to engage with this journal I feel certain that you have discovered new things that may have been buried deep in your subconscious. Hopefully, you are looking forward to a happier and more fulfilling sex life.

If you haven't already, you may find it relaxing to color some of the pages using pens or markers. I have intentionally left a blank page behind every page. But be sure to put a blank sheet of paper behind the page you are coloring to prevent bleeding onto the next page.

Thank you for buying my book. I truly appreciate it. If you liked this book I hope you will leave a friendly review on Amazon.

I am a very prolific graphic designer, writer, and a composer/recording artist. If you would like to view my offerings on Amazon here's how:

To see all of my books on Amazon please search for "Scott Shannon" in Books, and then click on the link "Amazon's Scott Shannon Page". I have more journal books as well as coloring books that include Sugar Skulls, Beatrix Potter, Tattoos, Dragons, Triangle, Hearts, Motivational Posters, and a series for gay men.

To preview my music albums, or single tracks, please search for "Scott Shannon" in Digital Music on Amazon. You can also find me on iTunes. If you want to save a bit of money on an album please visit http://ssdesigns.AmazingSites.US.

To check out my 350 designs on custom printed t-shirts please search for "Scott Shannon Designs" or "Toby Miller Designs" in Clothing. To see them categorized by topic visit http://ssdesigns.AmazingSites.US.

If you want to contact me please send an email to scott.shannon62@gmail.com.
I welcome all communications, except hate mail.

Scott Shannon

Printed in Great Britain
by Amazon